POUND @ GUANTÁNAMO

ALSO BY CLINT BURNHAM

POETRY

Be Labour Reading (1997)
Buddyland (1998)
Rental Van (2007)
The Benjamin Sonnets (2009)

FICTION

Airborne Photo: Stories (1999)
Smoke Show: A Novel (2005)

POUND @
GUANTÁNAMO

20 Poems, 2005–2014

Clint **Burnham**

TALONBOOKS

Talonbooks
278 East First Avenue, Vancouver, British Columbia, Canada V5T 1A6
www.talonbooks.com

First printing: 2016

Typeset in FreightText
Printed and bound in Canada on 100% post-consumer recycled paper

Interior and cover design by Typesmith
Cover art by Justin Lincoln via Flickr (Creative Commons 2.0)

Talonbooks gratefully acknowledges the financial support of the Canada Council for the Arts, the Government of Canada through the Canada Book Fund, and the Province of British Columbia through the British Columbia Arts Council and the Book Publishing Tax Credit.

LIBRARY AND ARCHIVES CANADA CATALOGUING IN PUBLICATION

Burnham, Clint, 1962–, author

Pound @ Guantánamo : 20 poems, 2005–2014 / Clint Burnham.

Poems
ISBN 978-0-88922-979-2 (PAPERBACK)

I. Title. II. Title: Pound at Guantánamo.

PS8553.U665P69 2016   C811'.54   C2016-901684-6

FOR JAMIE HILDER

"desounding is no consolation for concrete critics"

CONTENTS

II

the i who is spoken now is the speaker
the i who is speaking now is spoken

I'd like to acknowledge that we are on stolen land. I'd like
to acknowledge that we are on borrowed land. I'd like to
acknowledge that we are on pickpocketed land. I'd like
to acknowledge that we are on overdue land. I'd like to
acknowledge that we are on full land. I'd like to acknowledge
that we are on empty land. I'd like to acknowledge that we are
trespassing on someone else's property if that someone else
had property and if we are who we think we are and not, in
fact, perhaps also someone else's acknowledgement. I'd like
to acknowledge the knowledge of like to acknowledge you
like me acknowledging. I'd like to acknowledge I meant that.
I'd like to acknowledge I meant to say we are on land that was
emptied when my grandfather moved here in what was it, 1948?
I'd like to acknowledge my Dene sister. I'd like to acknowledge
my Gitksan brother. I'd like to acknowledge my Tsleil-Waututh
cousin. I'd like to acknowledge my Nuuchaanulth mother-
in-law. I'd like to acknowledge my Skwxwú7mesh daughter.
I'd like to acknowledge my Okanagan boyfriend. I'd like to
acknowledge we are getting into dangerous territory here.
I'd like to acknowledge that my grandfather moved here in
what was it, 1948 and then went back to Winnipeg and then
came out again with my grandmother and my dad and I'd like
to acknowledge I always hate it when I see the little items on
maps saying *IR30* but I also like seeing *IR30* – and it's usually
in italics for some reason – because they acknowledge how
they're little spaces marked *IR30* both part of the cities, of
human habitation, which are on the maps, and the landscape,
in time immemorial blah blah. I'd like to acknowledge the last
five minutes of colonialism. I'd like to acknowledge fifty pages
of postcolonial bibliography. I'd like to acknowledge the virtual
rez. I'd like to acknowledge the talking memory stick. I'd like

to acknowledge the suburban rez. I'd like to acknowledge the low-res rez. I'd like to acknowledge acknowledging. I'd like to acknowledge the brass mask my uncle made at reform school in the 1960s on Vancouver Island. I'd like to acknowledge the hot chocolate I had on army maneuvers on Skowkale land in July 1980. I'd like to acknowledge ... both I can't acknowledge and I'd like to acknowledge Oka. I'd like to acknowledge 518 years, four months, twelve days, seven hours, etc., of resistance. I'd like to acknowledge 10,000 years of resistance. I'd like to acknowledge the Freudian notion of resistance. I'd like to acknowledge British colonialism. I'd like to acknowledge Canadian colonialism. I'd like to acknowledge Musqueam colonialism. I'd like to acknowledge Roman colonialism. I'd like to acknowledge Norman colonialism. I'd like to acknowledge Persian colonialism. I'd like to acknowledge Franco-Prussian-Sino-Nippo-Indo-Afro-Turko-Islamo-Togo-Pogo-Hawaiian-Espresso-anyone-who-thought-they-could-grab-something imperialism. I'd like to acknowledge cultural relativist imperialism. I'd like to acknowledge academic colonialism. I'd like to acknowledge activist colonialism. I'd like to acknowledge poetic colonialism. I'd like to acknowledge that we are on bureaucratic land. I'd like to acknowledge drinking a glass of water ten minutes ago and not having to boil the water first. I'd like to acknowledge the ice on the inside of the walls when I lived in Labrador in the 1970s as part of the military occupation of Innu/Inuit/Indian land. I'd like to acknowledge not having mould in my son's room. I'd like to acknowledge hearing Elizabeth Goudie talk about her autobiography and working traplines in the '40s in Labrador in 1974. I'd like to acknowledge we are on stolen Stó:lō land. I'd like to acknowledge we are on messed-up Musqueam land.

I'd like to acknowledge we are on crappy Comox land. I'd like
to acknowledge we are on sexually harrassed Six Nations land.
I'd like to acknowledge we are on fucked-up Beothuk land.
I'd like to acknowledge we are on incestuous Inuvialuit land.
I'd like to acknowledge the triangles in the script and the
toboggans in the script in the phone book in Goose Bay. I'd like
to acknowledge the Ookpik Figure Skating Club. I'd like to
acknowledge corruption in the Department of Indian Affairs.
I'd like to acknowledge my word processing program just
capitalized the "i" in Indian just now and it did it again. I'd like
to acknowledge corruption in the hereditary chiefs and band
councils. I'd like to acknowledge corruption in the university.
I'd like to acknowledge corruption in the art world. I'd like
to acknowledge I was paid to say that, to write that. I'd like
to acknowledge the $750 I got from VANOC and the check
for which is in my wallet, right now. I'd like to acknowledge
that what I like about what I'd like to acknowledge is that it's
about me, a sensitive liberal, a tough but sensitive radical,
looking good, new T-shirt, do you like these jeans, they were
on sale, are they too tight, they were when I bought them
but now I need a belt, am I too old to wear this shit now, and
what I'd like to acknowledge is that I don't like it if I drink too
much. I'd like to acknowledge I was sober for four years and
I'm not now, I mean I'm not drunk right now but I have the
occasional drink or maybe more than the occasional drink but
I'd like to acknowledge I don't like it when someone reads a
poem about being drunk or getting cleaned up and they've got
the details about puking on their tits or that blinding feeling
in their head when they're suffering the morning after and
I'd like to acknowledge this is getting way too personal, even
for me, so I'd like to get back to acknowledging we are on

stolen, native, indigenous, Indian, injun, skimo, chug, Métis, First Nations, half-breed land. We are on native land, on native carpet, on native subflooring, on native foundation, on native weeping tiles, on native tarmac, on native sidewalk, on native dirt, on native leaf mold, the good mold, on native mud in our backyard, on native holes in the ground where our fence was ripped up by the landlord, not the landlord, guys working for a guy working for the landlord, maybe they were native I don't know, I didn't ask them. We're on native Highway of Tears on native land on home and native land and I'd like to acknowledge, I'd like to point out that we are the ones doing the acknowledging so you should give us a break. I'd like to acknowledge we're doing a lot more besides and could be doing a lot more besides. I'd like to acknowledge the acknowledging that we are on stolen, colonized, denied, dispossessed, unceded, ripped off, boosted, jimmied native land doesn't do a damn bit of motherfucking difference and I'd just like to acknowledge that.

DOOR OPENER

From John Bentley Mays to John Mayer
from axis of traffic to a six of evil
night: sirens warn not
want. Heavy healthy.
Murmur of voices can't
decide if TV, CB radio
or "actual" voices.
Wish piss. Heavy breathalyzer.
Wispish rustle of
corner stepkid.
Pages from provincial
physical exercise guide. Air
injected out from
nearby no stills.
Forefinger, index finger
ring finger (no ring)
thump on recovered
chesterfield "arm."
Sigh spoon in bowl
as bowl carried.
Okayyay. Suede pages
slide in boredom gesture.
Shakespeare in the dar–.
Overtown, tenderloin
Chinatown, uptown both men
wear checked shirts
both women wear
flat boots one
complains about
crack addicts telling
them this is their

neighborhood
before the ska show
outside the venue
but the next
day ten blocks west
an hour and ten
minutes before I
had to pick him
up from school.
he of the bored
stapled paper gesture
the next morning.
Neat be three fifteen
minutes after school
gets out and he and
his friends were playing
cops and robbers where
the black kid played
the cop and the white
kid whose parent is
a cop played the robber
and the half Japanese kid
and where the wood
chips stood in for
pepper spray later
an umbrella used much
as the Penguin used to
in *Batman* TV shows
but without the sleeping
Glas. Get hearts
pumping! Where in the

band meaning your
esophagus, affecting my
golf swing, pluck of guitar or
other stringed instrument
from another room: plung,
plung plung, plung.
Earlier in the week
accomplished with
big toe and index
toe to my chagrin.
Foot on coffee
table, no coffee on
coffee table foot on
guitar on guitar st-
and Stanley tools Stanley
garage door opener
girl bungee cording
Skilsaw to bike rack
atta girl between 500 gigs
and bagels foot
soldiers shoulder epaulette
as fashion item my
virtual Kitsilano mis-
heard as anti-Surrey
anti-racist rally before
he asked me if I'd
mind driving to Squamish
phone call during stroller
pushing she tears me
a new one during
playground keep an eye

out he offers me work
appalled at
dot matrix
on newsprint
ad beseeching work
for unemployed
Ph.D., Ph.D.
mis-spelled at
first, no, j-
ust incorrect use of upper and
lower case letters:
common mistake is to
refer to the Downtown
Eastside as the Lower
Eastside, but never
by an actual authentic
resident news announcing DERA
owes money according to
provincial gov't as I make
breakfast in a thunderstorm
of same, only
social workers, policy
advocates, artists,
academics, journalists,
morons, maroons, infidels,
pedophiles empty files,
single file, Indian,
file. By the rivers of Babylon?
Last man is shit so far he
fell the ones in front of
hair don't see him.

After getting home from the
Japanese noise concert
watch the *Battle of*
Guadalcanal but don't
catch the coincidence
till later, while reading,
arms folded behind
head, arm out-
stretched as if holding a
hammer, driving
in a nail. W-Mouth
made higher pitched noises
of airplane turning
five thousand feet in
the air. Bulbous
effect at
toe of sock slightly
loose, worn, stretched
pages on cushion
so head held with
cupped hand. "Stretched,"
"checked," "hearts,"
smeared on the page
"stretched" mirrored
on the blank page below
around "now"
from previous page when
closed to look for earlier
smeared words "of
socks," "the"
"nose" "P.H." "n"

"was" crossed out.
Crossed first written
as *drossed*.
Neighbor's footsteps
above my head and
then mock roaring at
toddler muffled words
like how I feel but
don't have to express it
but can't shouldn't
won't. Push-
button cappuccino machines
we used to pretend to doff
a cap to signal same
now they have small
digital clocks magnet
mounted thermometers in
the milk jugs and
arabesques on the
foam for Iraq-bound
soldiers at SFO
he writes my
name on the mug without
my asking versus I very
precisely pronounce my name
silently loudly to
emphasize both the "kuh"
and the "tuh" just now
out loud the "tuh" to
check for accuracy before
writing it down from

Tupperware to Avon Lady to
Book of the Month Club to
Reader's Digest to Eaton's
catalogue to Watkins to
Independent Order of Foresters
to DeMolay to Sisters of
Jehovah to fuckerware
versus Central America
Support Committee to
Anti-Apartheid to
Tipper Gore to Gore-Tex
to text me to Texicali
to Lieutenant Calley
DVDs stacked on VHS
cassettes on DVDs in
green box in front of
green basket next to
TV Wendy gave us covered
by deer rug that hung on
my wall 40 years ago
with VHS cassettes is on a
slant like the dotted lines a rabbit
explains football
strategy trajectory
white dotted lines to
Martian. See ya but
little no noise of
her leaving. False alarm.

CROSSING THE STRAIT OF GEORGIA

12-30-2013

grey shower cap black capstan
metalwork paint thick
as on plywood cupboards
Alberta 1970s PMQs

Bach's fugue by a 37-yr-old
string quartet, faintly
from an iPad in a tweed bag

black grey streaked
mercury water

mercury'd slaughter
aluminum, D said
the day before

as we hiked
over a beach
round a point
up the road
& down
to the Port Wash dock

a long time
remembering
the solar word

up the road
down the stairs
and a runoff
engineered to stop
at an old doormat

and two generations'
green'd cind'r block

(earlier, a beaver's
chewed tree
still standing
like a Warner Bros.
cartoon pencil)

(salal slapping
my Durangos
wettish in
miso
punchline)

a brass band
a brass bell
rope from clapper

solar panels on
empty boats rigging

a dump truck
cover pulled back like
a black window blind

yellow pipes
strip of paint

tears of rust
streak the white
metalwork
orange yellow brown

three small white chocks
ziggurats like an Aztec Ikea
shoved in a bracket
an orange one,
my foot's against

crenellated crit
icky surf
ant staircase
10-year wit

THE GULAG ARCHIE PROJECT

It isn't very funny.

If you laugh you're insensitive.

I always liked Ronnie
he had that Stalin look to him.

Moose would've been a KGB henchman
straight out of Le Carré.

Dexter? Well, a Party member of course. You should be afraid
of Dexter.

Jughead is Bakhtin
but the *goofy* Bakhtin
not the Goofy Bakhtin, that's his brother
toiling away in his dacha
did Bakhtin have a dacha?
look it up
making bowler hats into those clownlike ones he wore. I like
the pins on there.

My parents had *The Gulag Archipelago*
have to ask my father if he ever read it
along with other Book of the Month Club series like the
Sherlock Holmes collected stories, Pierre Berton's *The Last
Spike* and his Klondike book, and a two- or three-volume
biography of Lester B. "Mike" Pearson, even though my father
always voted Conservative.

The whole Betty vs. Veronica thing
lately resolved in Veronica's favor, from what I understand
was an allegory for the Cold War, of course, which means

Archie is the Third World?
And the Soviets won?

Did I say Ronnie up there, I meant Reggie of course.

Were there any black characters in the Archie comics back then?

What's Riverdale, a divided Europe?

When we lived in Germany
cockroaches in the apartment the French left us
they drank red wine in the air traffic control towers
this was in the '60s
everyone left their car gassed up for the wife & kids to drive to
Switzerland in case the Cold War turned hot.

What about the Choklit Shoppe? That's the VCR
pure consumerism, the libidinal desire of politics
that Fukuyama claimed really turned the tide and ended the
Cold War (and History).

There was that other girl, Dexter's girlfriend, she'd be the
dissident intellectual, afraid to make jokes over the telephone
"writing for the drawer"
passing around a *samizdat* manuscript of a play she'd never see
performed, some baroque mixture of Pasternak, the Beatles,
and Tolstoy:

    COUNT PIERRE
It's you baby, you're all I need.

    NATASHA
Pyotr, can't you see, I need to be free.

Clark Dewdney crosses a hotel lobby, receives a text from a 778 exchange.

Anonymous, but this doesn't bother him, he has his fans.

Wakes up hungover in a courtroom (former art gallery).

Can't we talk about the rentier and euthanasia, he declaims from the visitor's gallery. A major new architectural feature: two-inch thick raw concrete, with a finish as smooth as a dowager's dewlap. Wrap some cashmere around that crepe.

Meanwhile, Zagreb in Vancouver: snowboarders board buses, carrying two-fours of Lucky and smoking blunts as thick as a curling broom. The panhandlers eat Hamburger Helper in the alleys, posing 'neath two-pole power lines like flaneurs in flannel.

The more rush Ross Giotti gets from his custom tear-aways (how aughts!) – or at least I heard it on the DL from CL Smooth on his new "mix-tape" – leads to Clark on the SkyTrain, like it's the first time he took the El to a waterfront hotel.

But wrong waterfront – New West – with bike stores and shoe stores and Mugs and Jugs for feeling a copycat crime book at either the Sally Ann or the Army & Navy. You grab a brick of cheese, hop on the SkyTrain, and next thing you know you're in the Ivanhoe, peddling boosted cheddar to buy a jug of Bud. Look northward, arthritic angel, the archive is online, free, and utterly uninterested, but turned off after 10 p.m. to protect it from Russian hackers (how '80s! – as he found out from *Iron Man 3*).

HIGH.PARK

if.it.was

the year

of the day

or the time

of the season

not when

they shoot out

the window

&

miss pepper spray

or take the bus

Greyhound

to the battle

Sgt. Pepper spray

verboten, broken, self-denial

break my toe

sipping a latte

kick a pile

election monitors

stand

I have no voice

taped to

found in Ore.

Sears puffy

outside the entrance

to the gym

by the shop

she'll work at

now you know

the drill

full-court press

stat ASOP

to the max

old NATO protocols

are hard

to shake

problem isn't

so much react

to York work

you arent are

the boss

of my work

not the boss

of me jerk just

a suit

it were family

but on reactive

to my family

as if

it were work

a break through

a drive-thru

the fcuk-up

drives home drunk

mountie in a

rear-ender

into parked semi-trailer

murderer dick

were a drug,

thug huts

and lugs

bug

the dead

with bed eagle

Stetson head

many a hear

for the feat

that that fat

hat's la Tey'll

drag its tail

down to the

crotch of Kingsway

the cunt of Mount Pleasant

decrying gas & dash

or fag 'n' drag

or sip 'n' go

driveway drive

I's the b'y that

builds the cash cows

be *esse*

cash crop crap

that shit

tastes like shit

riding shotgun

shack from Knottage

to I glue

from frottage to

crowdsurfing plant

yourself there

porch fridge

ceremonial memory

foam and mesh

connects to now

says

but we're not white

atta boy

don't do anything

I wouldn't do

leaves you

quite a bit

of room

actually

actually

he gotcha'd

you can't

be good

be careful

get a good

lawyer

if you

ain't dragging your feet

to the bong show

why the binner

hunched over

his bulging

shopping cart

listening

to Cash

sing about the pony

dragged me

out of the fire

eyepatch tassles

Band-Aid tastes like

one 2 often

dunno

I gave the panhandler

who'd called me

a fucken asshole

a dollar

because she didn't

recognize me

(temp. –10°)

a good meal

does that to you

makes you unrecognizable

and charitable

a win-win

sin

situation

the b'ybridity

Frankenfoods

vacuuming the bottom

dry interior

of the province

just-washed

seems is opposite

of fucking

new straight

one inch

like a lot

    – paper

    – is another

    by Flav

    and church

    like Proust's steeple

    in MP

a paragraph

you have

to keep

rereading

a path

to

tretrace

the book

to find

your place

on the DVD

you can't

"bookmark"

that heritage "site"

it's H-O-T-E *HOT!!*

like ah said

son

they're using a machine

to do

what you don't need

a machine

to do

when wiggers

look in the

mirror do

Ɨ they sea

Melanesians

as origin

of reciprocity

rice-cooker gangster

gurgling sounds

like a skateboard

grinding go

around

the world sticking

branches into anthills

branching sticks

in my craw

why the parakeet

that's regional

vaginal

and culturally specific

meanings of subjects

and utterly diluted

and undermined

by mass marketing

he line ouch

Coach al Coach

Ivor giver

universal Coach

cash

getting go

all th way

to Paris

to see a ch

cash corner

ripe fist

history fight

they're always

clutching their ribs

chest funky

soul Thai

gambler wearing

indie uniform

shirt Schoolly D

as the classics

Pilipinas in jeans

white runners

bombers

puffies

hoodies

an illiterate thief

and swindler

or Marxist poet's

dictatorship of truth

fire the boss

W.A.S.P. wisps

wipes hands

as Slavs dance

formerly alienation

from labor

my bosses

doesn't alter

id unbought

and unbossed

no politics discussed here

from Mussolini

to water polo

from the get-go to the sack

illumination after

the explosion

would really make

the crap

a guy's gag

gone with the wig's

list to dog's

The Ten Commandments

for Little Children

why are the Sartres

always born

on the other side

do you like him

no

but I like him

even less

as an enemy

we were worried

about suicide

bombers flirting

with us

in Basic

at the 'Wack

gave you graveyard

shift sky

darker

ground bitter

donut cup

kale grows

in the cold

the garden

has snowed

over while

sobs and

red peels

no hard

feelings

I could hardly

make out

what you

were getting at

make yourself

useful

I shall

be making

viaduct

love to you still

waters run

tennis lessons

my foot!

fly off the handle

who's afraid

of the big bad

wolf pigs wanna

blow down my grow

whistle which

wolf

I mean

which hole

the pig eater

gentile/infidel

or girleater

not afraid of the shark

she's a man

eater leather uppers

when I'mmmm goodddd

andddd readyyyy

don't make your head

live act

you do the car

math bitch

cheat at the

letter of reference

never reaching

its destination

me is as if

the house

I overheard that

put you

should the guy

guiding the guy

trying to get his

big Chrysler

out from

in front

of the red Recovery Club

cats babe

on one of

the back tooth

first irised to

if you get the lumber

first

you're swimming

down the wrong

creek a second

kick of the mule

really *isn't*

educational tofu guy zone

always on the arm

standing in the doorway

with the '70s toes

of one foot

pigeoned

over the toes

of another Princeton's

meat draw

the East End Idol

don't minimize it

validate it

cups leather gloves

Dr. Asian guy

with wraparound

shiny black sunglasses

pink dress

shirt untucked

black leather

little bitty

mustache hair

to collar

ergo

a dissolute

T. Lee

current crop

of power pop

later: horses

pulling the car

flapper with cowboys

Model T in a

John Wayne movie

kid to dried triple-triple

medium-media

premature spray-on

suntan starter

fake & bake it

was a time

when they seemed

House of Commons

Parliament/Dre

possibilities

when Luscious Jackson

was fresh and new

tough luck LA

Polaroid sunglasses prof

proofed prefab

buildings to

manufactured homes

the unsayable

the salable

story where people

take home letters

afterword Science World

stalk Clit Eastwood

autobiographical police

operations

my grandmother's

clause

has

been superseded

Big Heat appearance coach told me to mail my write-up of the
step class by Tues. She said: Leave Vanc., go to your 12 step
reunion then wed Pinter's window in time for the Junos. If the
road rain rock leaves your truck 3 windows short try the Clipse
intelligence handbook in the glove box. The key point practice
is to leave a participle in the pratfall sequence unchanged.
Blackadder's method as desounding is no consolation for
concrete critics if they're called calloused but really, that's
uncalled for as asbestos removal is the best trick investors
can articulate. The best b'y sang a country & western tune
from the WWF soundtrack for karaoke. I want to type in
www but my tay battery is uncharged and the sink rust from a
sympathetic lesion made it hard to simper. Maybe in 1984 you'll
be taking the in- or outgoing 4-track lessons. He's thick and
mobility is not an issue, but ex-cited ballplayer bullshit is just
so many words.

Wagon on the sidewalk means the boys just left their false
cow on your choice for TV show. The Queen's address usually
makes the mofo brothers stay out till it's over, say, at Blanket
Fest. In Drumheler the drum machine was broken, thank god.
The RTM to ATM genteel goatee grated seamlessly vision of
crisis my ass action badge sewn additives

If normal ignoramuses volleyball board to death of sight
private creek provo pork machine PP sole home soon-ish
his hysteria her wisteria my widowmaker bat also Brando,
Clift, Misao D on upper arm p'raps for them into a desolation
consolation constellation prize this strains at your be slash see
the police station from FTW to WTF film still charged morning
not dead from VD to DVDs playing Hi Bob! in Clint's movie
knowledge transfer's expired in IN invisible peace movement.

Saying
I get it
keeps running
your teeth buck

farm to
fairly she was
talking about she
ain't my
family

Vermeer
leaf chipper
'78 Cadillac
limo so
mauve side

spiral Hummer
he said
I had
to fill out with

me lot-ay
not lat-ay him
ninh minh Prell
the boy

tell Torb's ha
Store thru the
moon sun
no
addled her

for
fell
ratio
the blame
the glampire
blobalized glimmer

of gun truth
these idea melle
pelle glue twins
from the
the girl

lost xi
stuck
produce that
free style
freeswirl less chalk

year grand
dump good'n
more talk
teak set
vibrate
to life

I old
stat pho
to as
failed all
the someday o
k pine
will

or was deserve
a tree not
all hugs
cone
one
or red needles

all hugs cone
one or red needles

cello
like diapers
look shoulder
pads half-
back naoya
Hotakeyama
is so
dimebagback's
ch335y
gordita inside
it the donor

walls ur-bun
the knuckle down
for a stadium in
a lab beaming
bulb, fo second get
suburbs in stadium

as 10th
our who
we
are for

a could
are-bure-boke

what just
think of
what we
ordered if
we Beckett's
three buttons done

on child's condo
twos aren't
11:15–12
yellow (amarillo)
up Pound's

Pluto 10:30–
11:15 blue
(azul) 9:45–
10:30 red (roja)
supereuropean

cover 9–9:45
green (verde) time
slots per color
shirt Lars on Me–

mag
cake
gate
to
brad

sluts
quilt
for
Cutter's
brother
was
my

boxing from raisin rape
to and kid will
end eerie youngest

from a
good fill
out sick
toy had a
teeth son's
god
father
choose

sketching us lose
you key Don
King sits on
a door
step-three teen guys

don't
discussion play
angry philosophical
eviction
thirteen disdain wall

hap
tick loud
song adolescent
not
Metallica so very
play is tree
your Grieg

a me drunk?
deserved
tell lab
state your
reverse cougar
failed did
constitutes

K'OMOKS

Brooklyn Creek

meowy xmas

woofy doyear

Millard Creek

Royston

Comox Logging Road

Comox Lake

Nymph Falls

Roy Creek

Trent River

Grassi Point

Spindrift

Union Bay

Dorothy Rd.

Ship's captain said he'd steam half-way 'round the world for a
   load of Comox #2 coal

Beaufort

Washer

Lansdowne

Hindoo Creek

Mar Vista

E&N

Buckley Bay

T'Sable River

Cougar Smith Rd.

Cowie (Cougar) Creek

Closed for the Season

Seasonal Fir

Bobcat & Septic

Frontage

Waterloo Creek

Rosewall Log Sort

Berray

Rosewall Creek

North McNaughton Creek

South McNaughton Creek

Sensitive Habitat

Cook Creek

Chef Creek

Thames Creek

Nile Creek

Spider lake

Horne Lake

Kinkade Creek

Little Qualicum River

Except Maintenance and Authorized Vehicles

Ocean Blue Plumbing

dirtbikes or quads

Whiskey Creek

Crocker Crab

Hi Al, Hi Tubbs

Bike route

Cross here when safe

French Creek

W. Morningstar Cr.

E. Morningstar Cr.

Bridge Ices Aircraft Patrolled

Wade Stewart Tree Service

No Hitchhiking Pickup is Illegal

Avoid Hydroplaning

Nanoose Bay Peace Camp

Bully's Turf Farm

Fredheim

Mid-Island

Kaspar

Nanoose Creek

Nanaimo Jim.Com

Barrel Creek

Lean-to on the lean-to on the Western Front

Susan Forrest

To report a forest fire call *55

Outstanding Ocean View Executive Home

False Gabriola symptom

Nanoose Overhead

Tsow-Wi-he-Nam

Snaw-Naw-As

Wancliff

Grey Sea

From Merville to Lantzville & back again

the Harbour City

Mary Ellen

Maranatha

Fukeneh or Fukenhi

Rock City

I KNOW WHAT'S COMING NEXT

Don't read this poem
Get your own comminuted dunnage
Old sunset applesauce applause Chris Chromosome
Yawning yacht rock O, MY, ALLAH
new and used bed for sale
make of that what you will
globalization has no balls
this is what a feminist's tits look like
makes ordinary people look like pro-am mascots
rutabaga for kumbaya (rooting beggars for kombucha
you betcha)
you caught me at a bad time: I'm
left arm tan working on his van
right winger from East Van
born to work, forced to rock
why wouldn't you expect anything else
Orange Crush and old blue new yeller
he can't do much inside of a truck: hence, DNA
sprigged fedora in front of me or a ball twister ought to be
wheel to wheel I'm out to some settee
bang on steel and hang some stool
samples here on the on the edge
from H. Rap Brown to Tapout
outside the Recovery Club
her scooter bedazzled
BlackBerry with studs
from bill bissett's iPhone
heavy stroller parking lot
homegrown da kine from resin to reign
tenure itch penitentiary
I'm just sayin' Twillingate of this *Twilight Zone*

Not wearing neighbor with fake books but real nipples
oh, *that* Groucho Marx mirror scene, see, I thought you meant
Frickin' fanny pack's retro not
Arnie's condom head
cut open the possum check for best-by date
Southern drip irrigation? legacy
men leap over where the hedge is lowest
shambolic as insult? AMS/PMS?
I don't think deniability is a swear word
you want to use to get a handicapped
parking spots are being phased out thanks to
disability studies becoming a program
with it own building near the Teflon
president's wheelchair ramp for coffins
officers of the neighborhood
black with war comes trappers
press one for genocide
two for sexual harassment
three to speak to an operator
where's reverse discrimination?
Wagnerhag a horse is looking for me
·aiming its nameplated gun
wedding invitation sprayed on gray plywood
smack between my tight buns
wipe-out's falsetto before they
inquired G. Lee's was real
(he does) thank you fact-checking
as a second language cuz
from soul patch to soul chip
the wire glass holders on the bowl
stramp ceremony

the Indian is a queen first, person second
fred & turks
catch my drift?
walking on snowbanks?
keep semi-chaotic penis
I'm gonna goods & services the good
freglancester
why Cadence Weapon left Friendster
why the Flava Flav transformer twins're buck-toothed
fanny pack worn w/ aplomb in Alphabet City
ol' *sixbuxsux* pin
no-name brand of the father's second wife's
literally, no, I mean *literally*
3 a.m.
Wendy & Mark's house
Wendy going to work
me watching *Happy Days*
Mark hasn't had any coffee?
I'm with the boys
weighing in on *Mister Rogers*
my dad's there
where is my blurb Jason black MEC backpack?
outside: kids shoeless and naked
other staff member kisses a rhino
three Remembrance Days
then it's election time
the building fantasizes we're inside it
the building comes as it finds us funding a new car
drawings and photographs on the same page: ancient
technology, cutting edge

fugly baby's makeover in *The Adoration of the Magi 2:*
Money-back Guarantee?
Who said anything about a fucking money-back guarantee for
frickin' frankincense?
prosumers' visitation rights pressing Prussian possum rights
don't want probablies
come strapped with a pamper my ass
hair on the cake
is itself
hair on the cake
is it self
Fordism
Toyotaism
punchbuggyism
SUVisn't
the short happy half-life of sport-ute
the short happy life of sport
the short sleep-slap-happy media ave of cigaret
if you say meo enough times it'll
remind me of meow mix16 master mike fright night wig sweats
mao, maow, neko
cub, cougar, corn sisters
before the coffin (six strong men), mixtape
mixtape about nothing's still about
I'm way behind the eight ball (and a trip to mexico after
the ICBC settlement we stashed our stash on the
boulevard before the cops got there) viz race
politics and digital inhuman
before he

Heart is sketchy so everything else is just told. Decide *Driving Miss Daisy* through the Huron torture scenes but without a Steadicam. There are no racist words for white man on Quebec near 15th. For one hour today we are all one people then we get back to the main business, which is earning like, likes. A picnic at Kiyooka's hanging tree, Webb was mad they mispronounced *ghazal*. Ask me a question but then I'll say your interrogating the Gateway to the North Star runners were my jam in the '70s, before I knew what a "jam" was, but it came in cans later used to store screws in, like a casino wheel with dozens of Gerber's babyfood jar lids nailed to 'em. Ask away. PG can mean born with a silver coke spoon in your mouth or *please go easy* or Prince George Eventually or the pig or a Skid Road, where four deer dance delicately between the highway, the Nechako, the Fraser there's her hair gel cutaway bank fourteen. A bandage's thread. So, should we refrain from telling white people how to dress (they won't listen anyway) out of respect for their cultural specificity, the DNA of yoga pants on Vancouver near 15th, the genomes of a loosened suit and tie, the backwards Blue Jays hat screwed on too tight for porn stud studies. My ex's off Thalidomide mouse pad hewing down a stone. Axe with a tree, real poets can Sharma sharpen a chainsaw in their Crocs, scrape the corrosion off the motor, get back into the water, check the crab trap & home for single malt the son-in-law left in lieu of diaper's Big Dipper. St. Paul's conversion to Betamax is the Pirate Bay, get jiggy with the giffy, the Amazon's one-breasted anesthetic anorectic poem, the 5BX at the Canex in Comox. Dropbox discovered litter-known kitty little end credit roll of history. Scuffed runners and socks drying on the airport carpeting. A truck dusted in road crud, a cowboy hat pocked face angry dark hoodie son with pizza, one woman with a walker another in a motorized wheelchair their caregiver in a scooter, I put the smokes between the papers so you know where they are, the Pepsi-Colonization of the north. Mr. Big on *Sex and the City*. The police at the bottom of the sea run out of gas. LNG. Don't bring your Anishinaabe theory to my territory for certs.

TRAGG'S CHOICE 2

you'll do fine

someday you'll be important

what you need is a drink and some lamb stew

what they've got upstairs is gas-station drip coffee

best shadow job I've ever done

incidentally it's got a bum tube – static is terrible

you keep feeling that don't you?

I'm glad you followed me

Wyoming, just you and your pal the doc

yeah I've always been a cornmeal man myself

how about you, you ready for surgery?

how we gonna look getting back to shy without a set of horns?

course, I suppose 20 years does make a different

we'll take you into Moose

well we'll get this straightened out and everything will be fine

and dandy don't forget dandy

3 a.m., time to call on a model

Compton Model Agency

you're the most wanted man I know

the Alps of the Americas, that's what they're known as

you're getting a little monotonous with the take-me-in routine

and I've watched you ordering dinner

now maybe we can put each other on the starting line, hunh?

what are you gonna do with your money Red?

set up a scholarship at Harvard

why don't you like me?

I I I gotta know, I gotta know real bad

the great Canadian ending – death by snowplow

let's go keep it company

ZUM LAZARUS

1

Laß die heilgen Parabolen,
Laß die frommen Hypothesen –
Suche die verdammten Fragen
Ohne Umschweif uns zu lösen.

Warum schleppt sich blutend, elend,
Unter Kreuzlast der Gerechte,
Während glücklich als ein Sieger
Trabt auf hohem Roß der Schlechte?

Woran liegt die Schuld? Ist etwa
Unser Herr nicht ganz allmächtig?
Oder treibt er selbst den Unfug?
Ach, das wäre niederträchtig.

Also fragen wir beständig,
Bis man uns mit einer Handvoll
Erde endlich stopft die Mäuler –
Aber ist das eine Antwort?

SOON LATHER US

1

lass D hi! I'll goin' pair of bowling shoes
last Dief men hype oh! S. Thesen
zouk divers Dump ten-forkin'
own oom's fife undo's lo! Sin

warm schlepped sick blue Ellen S. end
interred cries last M. Doerksen wrecked
4 end glue click Alzheimer B. Seger
trapped off homie's ohm Ross dirt select?

Warren league'd Dee scold? Liszt oof-duh
Answer hair nicked cans all muh tick?
odour tribe to her sell-by then unfucked?
Act, that's far need 'er track Tigg

Also fraggin' fur best and dig
peace man unsmitten eyin' her handful
err de end lick stopped fit to die mauler
hey Ray Burr pissed Dasein ant forth?

HOLD HER IN LISTERINE

Yets
Lets
Jets come Führer
Beg earwig rescind hoor
5 Juvie shower indent TUG
Invert the (pray) Fung
Is dirty Knee Gagun

woman throws head back & laughs

panhandler asks guy in a suit
10 what're you on *vacation*?
afternoon of a long weekend

Mine Eigner
Spur Spanish
That's Kurt Waldheim's
15 dirty shirt in the dryer
Firstly ("Why Fur?" 7-inch)
Hey urb vomit Injun huts
The Ferangi's calming un-ned
Fondle Al Zen's hang-up
20 skidding skateboard liquor store Ferguson up
Nick owned finger bang
warned about deleting emails
divorce folder oh man
I'm sorry no it's all good
25 just a lot of things going on

Naked um yogi's *gesundheit*
before the sneeze sure knock *Seinfeld*

griping Gerhard Seuss
Uncommon Out fuddy Fiddy
30 And there's a sight
Here (hear)

Hear Khyber Pass following
fur bound demonstrate Tolkien's cockney
Mackin' urban? FUBU? Fubar?
35 Zoo Station or WaaZuBee's or Zoo Bar or Kozmik Zoo
Soo station video Gus land
When Nimrod crowd source her
& Dan Denzel been gainin'
on Sam, (*Apocalypse ...*) Laurence, Idris

40 I'm someone who drills these tears
so fain outs Bertie diary

Mannuuh mannuuh do doo do doo do
Stoler her reason den sister insister
Oven lambs, Shawn waste
45 her S Bren it
Unregret sick Wilde stain
See out carob inter
dying wry N-hander
Eying with mass, signing Ort
50 Fund felt sent that's Dax so run hundreds
Meek hickory dats her
Then Hercs loaded landed with gas
Fine glands in drunk Olympians

dander swishes a tenuous sucking

55 Von heightened is much calm
   Denver volunteers the mother's forehead
   Darryl *si*'s a dwarf barfs knifes knives
   The *Geist*-er share meeting
   Dirt bike aqualung cooling your yets lets jets out
60 there room jogs yen early bird
   Dirty bird home Reno
   Andy faucet quell comedy past cod
   Quell anyhoo a gelded two-for
   Kodak to nook: any takers?
65 Nock tuft then open shorts & west
   an fit tenfold Indian deepen
   Eying jogger earns less loose fur belt
   I'ma tags on fox tumor or embossed
   And hard again bough Mendez Listerine

70 Mercy sez lez ends bends nicely
   & her shun Faber FASS
   rook farts sure gaining on
   eke mine her music humming
   fond Steve Austin
75 Felix Quincy very
   SO sagging Devin Davos?
   Won war worn warns Hang Tarot
   Andy Williams bungying godhead gay ad
   Andre's wine is sit forte
80 Hedwig prezi flops *Fortean Times* past
   ganging up on some sumbitch net gain
   I'm talking distraught Hey pervy
   Chrissake provost

Nig Andrews set un-dreck
85   Dammit eh son

Hoodman dragging his feet in get mood tread var
and forget (or Forget)
Dagword (or Dae Woo)
nipped out
90   the Himalayas lunch special
worn so fools annoy and her
Darren's in your navy get-out
nay out defrayed Desert Hawk Stern
Den weekend on
95   her under underwear hurts
a grin
since seedy Kinder Morgan
Hummels (kitsch? so be it)
after I'll slung adult

100   now's guard
shine to murder fryer
and fasten spots no I'm licked
I knew when
Angry when soldier tags me on Facebook
105   in the union four you wise
Angle fatty tribute I'm and herb biz
Hawk shore Deepak fooling gibe the gift of a .gif
Look at the sun on the ferry out there
Eight o'clock float plane in the sound
110   Cum round her invite a whore in
that's tribe Andes loop

is Thursday Fri. then
the bracket out stick two fells
and Furby *Die Hard V*
115 Invert bar forest own a Viletone
wasabi inner tube nasturtium
vice Naiad

(never woulda ended it that way
119 if I knew it was the end)

CYCLE LICK

eat grievances err snacks
call my ms. blue 2nite
Eastchester-y brunet
blonde bond brawl dat
married to the flash mob ttle
swipe dip 4 prox note harder
does he get pints in heaven 4
you have to work harder a li
then jostle someone use the
schwarzfahrer sausaging
the crunch eat a that mof
uncle Oedipus bathroom hat
Grrrtie's the lost-and-found gen
the boss of loss generating stop
her musk's grimskunk the keeping i
metope relief's ungirt open @ the s
Carrie's heavy makeup loot playa re
broiling day harvesters' Vietnamese ha
thread counter to better humiliate: perio
polished Polish face deeply etched drilled h
neoliberal Augustan Romans' nostalgia thin lips
neoliberal Augustan Roman's idea think cruel lips
Caligula's demand to enjoy yr palatial fellatio (virgin)
dig those rags Dogon's goatees piercings 'n' Snugglies or
Vermeer's footwarmer fetish *tronie* Tronna *Tron* traum. Air

spit the stream o' milk Myanmar
do me a deal oh underemployed
houndstooth scarf or *kaffiyeh* oh
four hour Viagra and –ified old j
bun *loco* mass –expectorate hon
it takes money to lose money ar
eat less POO patient's name:
our neighbors spotlight bull
there's no bumper I ❤ Nwe Y
Elizabeth couch alley of Phoeni
NJ, to partake of the parkade of
put the red in red state and bot
sovereign exception frenemy x and
gape @ WCW's Super *Vater* in a D
Vautron tealand get coffee fie omo
dollah meter longs miter benchmar
in sweet blogging right typing left the
populist and the academic and cemeter
Metuchen Metchosin the chosen *voisin* qu
judgment a of enjoyment a of tanned Fanta
from *Dwarf Puppets on Parade* to (Zizek's puppe*
Dump the workload on my scar tissue right here ick lik
aid squad inc. volunteer first Passaic of communist shade 4G
burritoification or burrofication retro fitness Barack trading ok
post when the weather acts up he xxoo's unisex picken chic transit

the white man's unburden jersey
early nothing batman rat boy m
jewish lobby Christian atm mu
parking garage atheist garbage
free market waiting room agno
kitchen pagan alcove cat woma
the boat turned back for a tor
her heart in her mouth her hu
hypocrisy the nearest we'll g
pha-wagon boys scarf kye int
my mom's punch cards from w
the mountain 3 decades later I'
back at where I was standing th
from 29 years earlier she was st
about how she'd joked she might
before I left for SLC no longer sen
N later I'd work on the manual for
for instance met Penn reverse engine
Billboard charts I ♥ haters orgasmic toe
organic toss salad leak drank you *sure* you
in data storage starage steerage before she
gimlet never thought the beam in his eye'd be like
12x12 up across the painting roof beam after a hurrica
take it to CVS/pharmacy take it to Duane Reade take it to
it's 10 a.m. and I'm in Nolita (RATS OHON) cow rose riot letter
slide & divide demo reel highlights reel ouse girl n thumb as she
Highlights intersection Goofus and Gallant slim elevator Buddhist aint

the two superegos of my child
cot com relief is just around a b
whole *sole por* mayo getting t
no tenured Joan Crawford's *A*
Frank's signifiers (Reggie: let
miss mister myster transpare
the particleboard principle *Do*
boats *Official Detective Cross*
'er in DRIVE & the *Open Road*
ca. 198_ Dot's first poem the t
Red Sea the Red of the face Sg
Gantian Gnatiot assemblymen
what do you grab scrab cruelle
school of and art CBS studio's w
NB note Styrofoam crosses hand
TN go hand in hand technology a
the dormant demand to orange whi
eyebrows we annoy their enjoyment
the views intersection he enjoys christ
men moving engine block to save sinners
christ died pawn shop cum InSite shooting
gallery's the place for our sins shoeshine hood
two stickers play dot lock away o no rapped Hested
ground play man's *Woman's Face* blowers & Jim Crow
Tony's Vik's dust me be frank) don't old Glory hole beyond
Jeannette's hands *wnbeat word* put anarchist mag vern as the
Rodin's hands of god AaVsE rs politics solution for bigotry p spit

rocks the Sicilian curl &
cradle to knife throw not
grave two eat out of enjoying
bag Baudelaire's movie other
florist window Delacroix's
siphoning fuel horror of disposal
the void figures on the corridor
nature sidewalk bathers
ungainly footlights virtue
art director's creepy wheel
double bass violin chair
casino dino family tiles ram
top hat *qua* music stand other
improvised tarp as engine sling
feet as picture rest rock pile
return, Nick Lowe! watering can
Camille's creepzoid neighbor harsh light
house of cracked wall's Cézanne's popcorn movie
scotch plaid blue sky who knew grandmother net via
had a stash *and* downloaded? Homeland Security wheelchair ramp

NEWFAGS DON'T EVEN BOTHER LOOKING IT UP YOU'LL HATE IT

(from Prodigy's "The Big Gun Down" to *Speedball 2*)

RIP Richard Joseph :(martinstatic 3 years ago 34 Ice Cream !.... Ice Cream ! ZroDfects 9 months ago 33 One pussy is afraid of the speedball!^^ ToughGuyver 1 week ago does anyone know where I can listen to the gameboy version of this song? It's on a whole different plane :D.Ycarli 2 months ago @MrLarodos ... GET READY !! ZroDfects 3 months ago @ZroDfects REPLAY! MrLarodos 3 months ago @ZroDfects lmFAo..... i remember that XD :)) REDHALFOFMERSEY78 3 months ago Some of the samples are so quiet you can hardly hear them in this clip, but a classic tune.. MrSpudgun 3 months ago @dvega1 What? He died? plasmaarmelund 3 months ago @raigon1 Get the Protracker module and convert it to midi notes. emilen2 5 months ago dont know does many know this but there is freaking nice trance tune of this intro made by rinkadink track is named Marauder goatatti 5 months ago Dem were the days, British studios at the top of their game, so to speak. Mental techno music too. Now i know why i loved it so much. Loved how the uplifting chords break in once you near the end of the level. pure genius. thewotsit 1 year ago 16 NODE ACTIVATED... EXIT OPEN...LEVEL COMPLETE BitchinVR6 3 months ago 9 Video Responses This video is a response to Amiga Music – The Chaos Engine see all All Comments (24) Sign In or Sign Up now to post a comment! This ... is god ToughGuyver 2 weeks ago The 90ies - Good Times ToughGuyver 2 weeks ago Muss ich mal wieder zocken. Danke! ToughGuyver 2 weeks ago Chaos Engine!!!!!!!!! Geil!!!!!!!1 ToughGuyver 2 weeks ago @ ZroDfects what good is a 360 if you can't blast Chaos Engine on it Best Music on the Amiga 500. DantheGermanGamer

2 years ago 31 agreed. Ooh i remember this! Takes me waaaaaaaaaaay back. What a great game that was and damn that music is nice! Wish i had an Amiga so i could play all these awesome games again, they still are better then the games released these days. It actually took some skill to finish it. :P Frank00079 6 months ago 4 amigaaaaaaaaaaaaaaaaaaaaaaaaaaaa-aaaaaaaaaaaa.. happy years.. alloleo 1 month ago 2 see all All Comments (29) Sign In or Sign Up now to post a comment! Still got my Amiga,an it still works!!! :) Evolution5man 5 hours ago @gnamp Great advice! Downloaded it last tuesday and have been playing since. :) Frank00079 3 days ago in playlist Favorite videos @Frank00079 you may be pleasantly surprised to learn that you can play all these games again and more- very easily too... look up "WinUAE" and good luck :) gnamp 1 week ago nice touch!!! love the buy screen. Xenon 2 MB way best amiga theme, right before turrican 2 desert rocks.. DiabloManiacz 1 week ago @Frank00079 get winuae estebann 2 weeks ago @Frank00079 You can, use an emulator KDCW3534A 2 weeks ago Videogame system of the future : Amiga hackshield3 3 weeks ago this is the theme of John Carpenter's Assault on precinct 13 !! 4n7oyn3 3 weeks ago bitmap Borthers And Team17, killers of Amiga Games Destronr 3 weeks ago Great tune! The original is made from "Bomb The Bass" - very cool though if you think about the good old times and the old technology! ;-) Strap1205 3 weeks ago redcommando2 2 years ago Top Comments Never thought I'd hear this tune again. God bless youtube! hayabusa1x 2 years ago 39 see all All Comments (60) Sign In or Sign Up now to post a comment! wow this is like the best sound + music that i ever heard . i really have to dl more amiga music and 8+16bit thats where the gold ist ;) torstn 1 week ago This tune..

The torrent of memories!! When we played this game, I always took the jeep! It was.. my thing. =) HS6000 1 month ago best ever programmed music on an 68000 !!!!! suported of course , by the incredible sfx-power of the whole cbm-amiga series !!!!! XXplaythegamesXX 1 month ago Remarkable! AleksiGrobonow 1 month ago Hey folks, I can't believe this has been uploaded. I wrote the music to this game back in 1990, it was my first gig as a games composer back when I was just a wee 17 yr old. They paid me £350 and 2 copies of the game! It was written on Noisetracker and now I cringe at a few of the not-quite-in-tune samples, but at the time there wasn't any way of tuning them. Suffice to say I still score games, we started a little FB page a few months ago, come say hello, look up Bob and Barn on Facebook! barnage5 1 month ago 9 This song is excelent!!. lpgccarlos 3 months ago Cheat time 8) Pause game and type NCC-1701 Screen flashes and you have unlimited lives. fantastic song... I remember when I was kid – I recorded it several times loop to tape recorder and played constantly :) djnykk 1 month ago aledbutcha 3 months ago i have this game on my amiga 500 but it doesnt work anymore :(NukeCorruption 4 months ago PAULA = one of the best sound chips ever designed in computer history. JayArgonaut 5 months ago @melomonster007 Me too! lol JayArgonaut 5 months ago weaselfierce 2 months ago One of the best if not the best run and gun game ever made staybeautifulSB 3 months ago Amiga had the BEST music back then, C64 was superb but Amiga took it to another level that even SNES nor Mega Drive could keep up. cloudskipa 1 week ago Anyone ever surprised how well the gameboy version of this games soundtrack came out? One of the better 8 bit compositions of higher quality songs PifferyGear 1 month ago HEY! Nice!

I was actually going to upload something similar to this! Good stuff! :D SaxdudeMaloyS26 1 year ago @lardrat Chaos Engine had position-sensitive music, that is to say that it mixed in different beats depending on whereabouts in the level you were. I believe that this music is just a rip of each of the individual tracks all mixed in. sasfcps 4 months ago awesome game music good old days icykooldragon 4 months ago This was my favourite amiga game growing up !! Still play it on emulators >.< I started a fan page for Dan Malone (the artist on this game) on facebook recently, and via various links and posts I managed to contact Dan himself to talk to him about it, he was very touched his work was still loved...I mean, his work is classic! He even started to upload concept sketches from The Chaos Engine and also the original arena design for Speedball 2. Search for The Incredible Art Of Dan Malone on facebook was heißt indiziert? immer noch gut das game fairman1000 1 year ago fliehende Leute töten? soviel zu spielen so brutal.... ach indiziert? na dann ^^

HASHTAG@GITMO

sooo-ooo generous!

my gender workstation playdate
I don't know but I've heard it said
where do people in China get *their* cheap shit made?
my ethnic slaystation classmate
spreader nose frogger
fire guys suntancity Ruth's Chris anti-John Kerry song after
Obama won
straight for pay
chicane seatstand flamingo

the full Nanaimo vs Canadian tuxedo
Lynn Valley tux Ladner sports coat Cumberland dinner jacket

the lonely planet
the gregarious asteroid
the co-dependent moon
the overtaxed sun
the burnt-out star
the shunned dwarf planet
the anarchistic gravel
the laptoplugging pavement
the fax machine dropping curbstone
the racist overpass
the homophobic bush
the sexist but in a charming because unwitting way grandfather
clock

the dotting the i's and crossing the t's anal-retentive why did
you put apostrophes after the i and t manhole cover I mean
personhole cover that the class traitor sticks his head out of

during Jacques Becker's *Le Trou* before returning to the prison
to better betray the fellow prisoners so they can be stripped
naked in a final act of abjection and humiliation

there's no terror in team
there's no *terroir* in terror
there's no error in terror
there's no tremble in temblor

he sat next to the woman who was the mother-in-law
from sunglass station to sin less

twelve thirty o'clock tank stand
noseworthy hittin' a magilla gorilla circle wheelie
can you believe how technical that is
no shitting below the bibleborschtrustbelt

Java teaching my kid
about how the Puritans dealt with *Roe v. Wade*
in the second of every in American
sushi the hide-bound caribou

First Nations preservation stickee the highlights
front side of the bike potato picker bar hop unhiding
thumb wars to button mashing thanks Jase

I saw my name
in blue cursive script
on his neck
as she smoked
as he smoked
and his girlfriend
with a ponytail

beckoned to him
from the front of the bakery
he couldn't enter
biche
was smoking
and so he shook his head
Jove shook his dreadlocks

most physically endowed enduring
XQR: extreme quadriceps relapse

El Segundo LA
from Burquitlam Plaza to Redondo Beach metro stop

Bush with Burqas for the BU
Bush with bpNichol for the IT (umm, H)
Bush with a swastika for the US
my Viet Cong horse collar beer
quick sac loans for the wealthy com

sighing as air
wheezes out of hydraulics
he pulls gloves on
walks back to the back of the bus
where trolley wire has dropped

defeatist feed us de featus
from Dayglo Abortions to Women against Pornography
Jews against Zionism blasted pork rinds
heel click stripper a modification of the dandy candy bar

roman jakobson on i like ike
good cop goodie mob deep end

bad cop color me badd
hey virgin surgeon:
you snooze through snooze alarm
i lose arm

absolute Absolut
after me in angora
my house guest look back
hunh? can you tell me that
mr. canada arm
planetization jakes hoarder?

pot mouth potty month
the bus sits with stanchions folded back resting on its roof
praying mantis wings or fire arms

and anyways where will they make condoms after peak oil take
that to your one child family policy ops thinktank
zero tolerance population grown buy a Chinese baby

i was just thinking of dating the bush doctrine
what do you bring her I went to the door and rang the bell

smoke 'em if you got 'em excuse me you can't smoke here
thank you for not Bogarting
i never met a metamorphosis who didn't hope for spare change
hot dog vendor Buddhist jokes steer into the skid row

but don't leave tire tread on his clothes
there's a Windsor Plywood
in Burnaby is there one in Windsor too?

imagine oneself a wood-grain panelist

mind your p's & q's making it pdq
an instant eggnogy drink
Louis can't see Andrew's not there,
Gerald won't talk to me so ... I dunno

and then get back to me asap, USAF

U can imagine how I'd dress up as
Dolly Parton but I can't imagine why U'd
dress up as Linda Ronstadt

karaoke strip bar without the machine or central heating
funny as long as you didn't have to be there
that was a mildly favorable review

you know there's no I in team
there's no we in team
there's no forensics in team
there's no athlete in team
there's no middle manager in team
there's no teamplay in team
there's no I in family
wait ...
but you know what i mean
there's no U in family or friendship
yes, but there are two in grudgefuck

carpal town 'n' totem
carpool afflictions
skin-deep things we can do without

AD spaz lotus macula CAU skyline OZ ghost dance times
have you ever noticed there's no bald tall guys

lonely short guys get bald
and wear hats to look taller & so women can't see they're bald
go local or go home

be all you can just be yourself
no child's behind left behind
put the late in legislature

Hosni Mubarak is my joy.
George is kind and good and beautiful.
George is a success.
Hilary Clinton is peaceable.
Jack Spicer and a resemblance.
Dear me Hosni Mubarak is so kind.
Hilary Clinton is so kind.
George is gratifying.
Hosni Mubarak makes a sound.
Hosni Mubarak all around.
Hosni Mubarak is so dear.
Hosni Mubarak is so near.
Billy Little is not so kind.
George quietly.
Hosni Mubarak is necessary.
George necessarily pleases the latter.
Hosni Mubarak is an exercise.
Jack Spicer is so strong.
Hilary Clinton is such an experiment.
George is so warm.
Hosni Mubarak is so simple.
You mean Hosni Mubarak is all right.
Hosni Mubarak is mean.
Billy Little is so careful.
George.
George is all there.
Hilary Clinton is so impatient.
George is so clear.
George is so consecutive.
Hosni Mubarak is so kind.
Billy Little is so kind.

George is so kind.
Hilary Clinton is so sweet.
Billy Little is so satisfying.
Hosni Mubarak is so able to be praised.
Hilary Clinton is so able.
Hosni Mubarak is a picnic.
Sharon Thesen is so a measure of it all.
George to me.
Hilary Clinton is such a windmill.
Sharon Thesen is so strong.
I have no use for Maxine Gadd.
Maxine Gadd try again.
Hosni Mubarak is so soothing.
Hosni Mubarak is so strong and yet waiting.
George is so strong and willing.
Anne Stone is so strong.
Hilary Clinton is right.
Hosni Mubarak is so kind to many.
George is so kind to me.
George is such exercise.
Hilary Clinton.
Hosni Mubarak is so kind.
Hilary Clinton is so necessary.
George is so kind.
Maxine Gadd is so scarce.
Jack Spicer is no joke.
Jack Spicer is so kind.
Hosni Mubarak is such an incident in one's life.
Jack Spicer is such an incident.
Hosni Mubarak is hilarious, gay, and favourable.
George is courteous.

Hosni Mubarak is an occasion.
There is an instant of George.
Sharon Thesen again.
Billy Little together.
Sharon Thesen is anxious.
Jack Spicer is good.
Sharon Thesen a terminus.
Hosni Mubarak is so high.
Jack Spicer is delightful.
Use the word Hilary Clinton is so high.
Jack Spicer is so high.
Hosni Mubarak high.
Billy Little is all there.
Hilary Clinton is not very interesting.
Maxine Gadd has charm.
I am so discouraged about Hosni Mubarak.
About Hosni Mubarak.
Hilary Clinton is no joke.
Jack Spicer is so cold.
I say Hosni Mubarak is so strong.
What do you say about Barack Obama.
Billy Little is so strong.
George is so accurate.
Hilary Clinton is so erroneous.
Hilary Clinton is alright.
Maxine Gadd is amiss.
Hosni Mubarak.
Gertrude Stein.
Billy Little.
George is so strong.
Hilary Clinton and roses.

Clinton Burnham.
Did you say, oh George.
For Hosni Mubarak not to Hosni Mubarak.
For Hosni Mubarak.
What did you say Billy Little.
George how are you George.
Maxine Gadd.
I said it I mean George.
I said Hosni Mubarak.

ACKNOWLEDGEMENTS

"No poems on stolen land" is for Teresa.

"The Gulag Archie Project" is for Nicholas Galichenko.

"North by Pacific Northwest" is right after Jeff Derksen.

"HIGH.PARK" was written Toronto–Vancouver, March 2005.

"All the plumber's crack in Drumheler" was written on the Ides of March, 2010.

"K'omoks" is for Peter Culley.

"Zum Lazarus" is by Heinrich Heine.

"Hold Her in Listerine" is after Hölderlin (like, *way* after).

A note on method in "#egypt #jan25": I was asked to contribute to a special George Stanley issue of *The Capilano Review*. I generated a poem in which I reproduced every line with the words "lifting belly" in the first ten pages of Gertrude Stein's poem "Lifting Belly," as published in the Library of America 1998 edition. I replaced that phrase with the names of poets or public figures, depending on how many lines the phrase appeared after the previous one. Thank you to Maxine Gadd, Sharon Thesen, and George Stanley for agreeing to let me use their names in this poem.

"The Gulag Archie Project" was rejected by *Poetry Is Dead*. Other poems appeared in *Event, Abraham Lincoln, Open Text part 2, West Coast Line, The Capilano Review, UE*; thank you to the editors. Thank you to Jeff Derksen, Rolf Maurer, and Shazia Hafiz Ramji for the editorial assists, and to the staff at Talonbooks.

Clint Burnham has written books on Steve McCaffery, Fredric Jameson, and the Kootenay School of Writing. His books of poetry include *Be Labour Reading*, *Buddyland*, *Rental Van*, and *The Benjamin Sonnets*. He is also the author of the short story collection *Airborne Photo*, and the novel, *Smoke Show*. Burnham writes often on contemporary art and teaches at Simon Fraser University. He lives in Vancouver and roasts his own coffee.

PHOTO: LINCOLN CLARKES